Aconcagua

Stone Sentinel

Stephen Platt

www.leveretpublishing.com

Aconcagua: Stone Sentinel

First published - April 2002
This Edition - September 2017
Published by
Leveret Publishing
56 Covent Garden, Cambridge, CB1 2HR, UK

ISBN 978-1-9124600-8-3

Aconcagua

Aconcagua 2002

The route:

Fly Buenos Aires –Mendoza; Minibus to Punta de Vaca; Walk/climb, 14 days of ascent, 2 days descent to Puente del Inca; Drive to Santiago

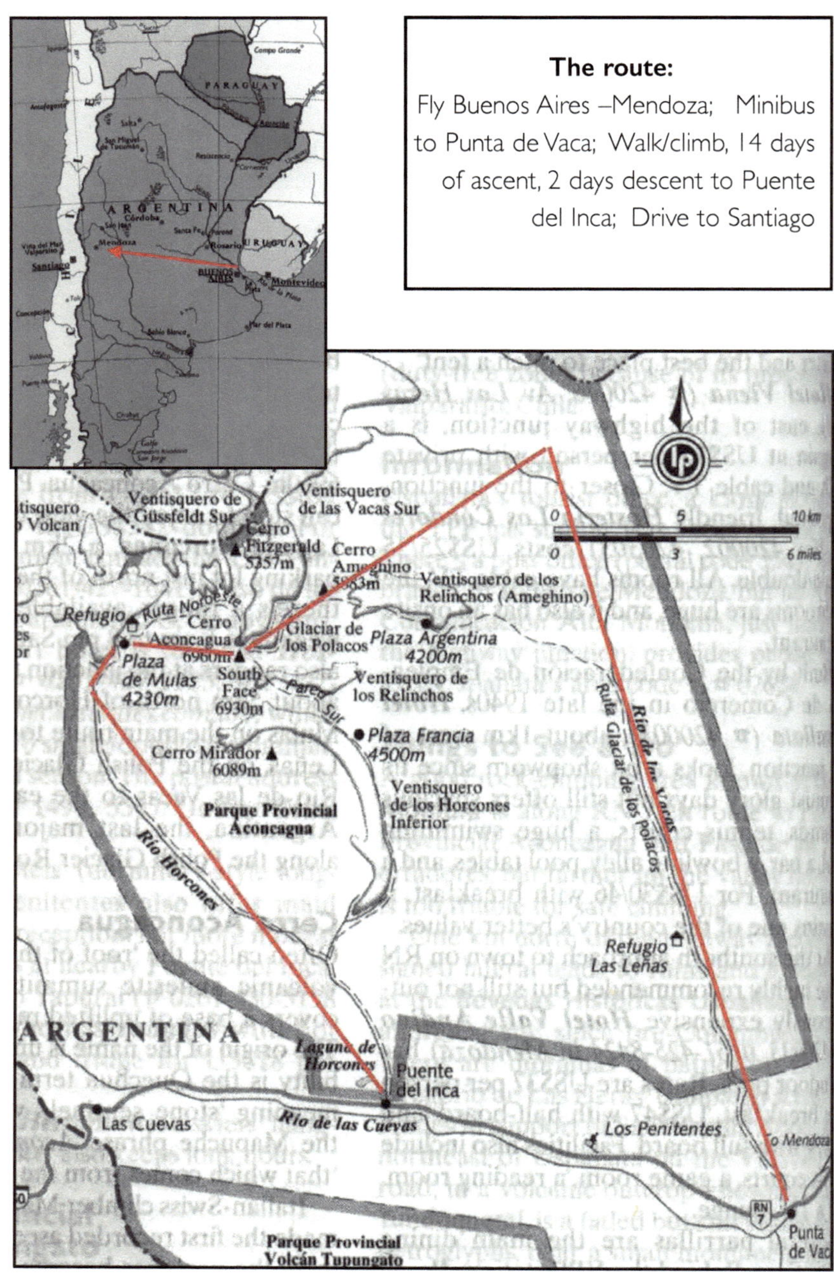

Buenos Aires

30/1/02 - London to Buenos Aires

Having slept fitfully on the plane from London to Sao Paulo I have less than an hour to make my connection to Buenos Aires. There is a crush to get off the plane as disembarking passengers fight their way past people going on to Rio who have stood up to stretch their legs. A young woman waits at the top of the ramp to shepherd us to the next plane. I ask her about my luggage. I've been coping with a nagging worry that there is too little time for my luggage to make the transfer. Anxiously, I try to catch sight of my duffle bag, but we are whisked away by another brisk woman and rushed to our next plane.

The two stewardesses claim to speak English, but can't understand my question. Finally the purser seems to understand. He takes my ticket and goes off to check. A minute or two later he comes back and tells me my bag is on board. I begin to relax.

Andy Paz, Manager, Argentine Office Cambridge University Press.

The captain tells the crew to prepare for take-off. Across the aisle the stewardess takes her seat. She is small, fat and bespectacled and looks liked someone's auntie, rather than the Brazilian goddess I'd been expecting. Preparing for take-off, instead of checking the passengers' seat-belts, she performs a little ritual of crossing herself, closing her eyes and whispering what may have been a Hail Mary.

Emerging from customs into the main concourse of Ezeiza, the international airport in Buenos Aires, I am immediately besieged by men operating as agents for taxis. They are so assured and direct that it is hard to ignore them. I find the bus company's desk, buy a ticket and am then able to fend them off.

After a rest, Andy Paz, manager of the Cambridge University Press (CUP) office, picks me up at the hotel and takes me to dinner at an Italian restaurant in Puerto Madero. We talk about Argentina and the current crisis. She thought that the main problem Argentina faced was deep-seated corruption. The taxi-driver I used the following day also said the problem was down to incompetent and corrupt politicians. But he said it was everyone's fault, including his own, since they had let the politicians get away with it.

31/1/02 - Buenos Aires

I walk through Retiro to the Biela, a traditional and delightfully spacious café opposite the Recoleta Cemetery, where I have a coffee while I write my journal.

Eva Peron's tomb is not that easy to find. I'd asked directions to the Duarte family tomb from the women collecting money for the blind at the entrance. But the cemetery is a city in miniature and I had to ask directions twice before I found it. Compared with some of the more flamboyant edifices, the Duarte tomb is relatively modest. The brass plaque has choice extracts from her speeches, which Tim Rice recycled for the lyrics of the musical Evita. From

Eva Peron QEPD 1952 26 de Julio "No me llores..." Don't cry for me.

there I walked through parks and past the British Embassy. It is barricaded like a fortress with high shuttering and cameras but without any sign of a Union Jack.

I am on a mission to try as many of Buenos Aires's famous cafés as I can and the next on my list is the café bookshop Clasico y Moderno. I cross the street to a Lloyds Bank, but the doorman tells me they only change money for clients of the bank. Outside the bank, waiting for the lights to change, two police cars screech past with their sirens blowing. Something has happened just where I crossed to the bank. More police cars scream to a halt, blocking the traffic. Whether a mugging or a murder, I decide I've missed it and that I won't go back.

The bookshop is a delight – lots of good books in a glazed two-storey annex to the café – soft lighting, polished wood floors with a metal staircase to the gallery above and old hat boxes piled in a corner.

I decide to stop for the 'executive' lunch – an all you can eat salad bar, plus pasta. The piano music I've been enjoying is live jazz. The architecture is amazingly Spartan. The plaster had been hacked from the walls, exposing the bare brick and concrete pillars. There are ancient steel roller blinds above big shop front windows and a suspended ceiling of steel reinforcing mesh. The atmosphere is created by the ochre brickwork, polished wood and floor tiles polished to a deep red lustre.

Outside, the sky is turning grey and I wonder if it will rain again like yesterday.

Cafe Clasico y Moderno

I didn't discover until I reached Av. Cordoba, when I checked my compass, that I had been walking north instead of south. Rather than retrace my steps, I find a different way to Avenida Florida.

A crowd has gathered outside a money exchange. Dozens of people are staring at a large screen displaying the latest dollar exchange rate. It doesn't change but the people keep staring. The official rate today is 1.3. The newspaper I'd read over lunch argued that the proposed rate of 1.8 pesos to the dollar was a panic measure. The rate on the screen is already 1.6.

Consulting my map to avoid making another mistake, I pull my passport out of my back pocket along with the map. Subconsciously I hear it slap on the pavement, but would probably not have noticed had not two different passers-by pointed it out to me. For the next ten minutes I give thanks to the gods for rescuing me and make my way to Plaza de Mayo where I hope to see the 'Mothers of the Disappeared'.

The mothers form a line, holding a blue banner which proclaims their resistance to state terrorism. They march in a wide circle around the centre of the square. I sit on a bench and watch. They march every Thursday afternoon to

Madres de la Plaza de Mayo

demand a reckoning for the thousands that disappeared during the so-called Dirty War in the seventies. On the Avenida de Mayo there is a small demonstration of workers protesting the current crisis. There are more police than demonstrators and I wonder if they are over-reacting until I pass one boarded-up bank after another. From here it's only a short way to the Café Tortone.

The legendary Café Tortone, founded in 1858

The Tortone, the most famous café in town. Huge and Victorian - maroon red pillars support a high corniced ceiling and the glimmering bar supports an ancient painted cash register. The deep space is lit by soft wall lights and stained glass ceiling panels. At the far end of the café, a wooden arch, like the choir screen in an English church, separates the café proper from the billiard tables where two young men are playing under painted chandeliers.

At the corner of Avenidas San Martin and General Juan D Peron a screen in another exchange shows 1.85 pesos to the dollar. But their doors are locked and their tills closed. Maybe it's the time of day, but the streets are full of armoured cash wagons collecting money.

Avenida Florida is pedestrianised from Avenida de Mayo north to Plaza San Martin where I'm staying. It is thronging with people. Halfway along a striking looking man with a beard sings a Latin American lament. He is seated, playing a guitar. His face is so commanding and his voice so strong that it is only after a while I notice the crutches under his chair and his withered legs.

Towards the top end of the avenue a troupe of tango dancers are warming up. A man in a trilby, who has been announcing the performance, begins a mock dance with a younger man with slicked black hair. Then the men take it in turns to dance with their female partner while the other works the crowd.

She is blonde and wears a tight black snake-skin skirt over bright red fish-net stockings and high-heeled shoes. Her skirt rides up when she lifts her leg and leans back and we can see her matching red knickers.

Tango in the Avenida Florida

I catch a taxi to Andy's flat and she takes me to a restaurant by the river, called Tango. I get back early and sleep reasonably well, rising before 6 to grab a coffee before taking the taxi to the airport and the flight to Mendoza.

1/02/02 - Buenos Aires to Mendoza

The domestic airport in Buenos Aires is a surprise - a spacious, modern, genuinely good building.

From the air the River de la Plata is a wide brown shallow sea that ends abruptly in two thin fingers which extend into a seemingly endless green. Beyond the city limits the county is divided into green rectangles like a very difficult jigsaw. Just before Mendoza the Andes appear - there seems to be a lot of snow.

At the hotel reception, I telephone Rodrigo, director of Adventuras Patagonicas, to tell him I've arrived and go to my room. I wait an hour or so before a girl arrives to check my gear. As the day wears on, I learn that our party of ten is one of three groups climbing the mountain. There seems to be some doubt about our chances of doing the Polish Glacier and I wonder about trying to clarify this but decide to wait and see how things go.

I spend the afternoon wandering around Mendoza, getting lunch in a nice café and walking from plaza to plaza, sitting on benches waiting for the day to cool. But it seems to get hotter and hotter and I go back to the hotel to wash. Rodrigo appears at the evening briefing and we go out to dinner at an open air restaurant and started to get to know each other.

2/2/02 - Mendoza to Penitentes, 8,500'

I wake early and after breakfast go out to telephone Scharlie and change money. On the way back with time to kill, I stop at a pavement café. Two tables are occupied by men reading newspapers. I order a coffee and watch the passers-by in the warm sunlight. The waitress brings my order saying 'cortadito grande', literally a big little coffee. I stop again on a tiled bench in the Plaza España to watch the world go by. Expeditions are all about hanging around.

Back at the hotel the luggage is being loaded onto the roof rack of a mini-bus. After a false start, when some people remember that they've left their passports in their bags on the roof-rack, we drive to the Park Rangers and hang around an hour while they enter our details on their computers.

We drive through dry broken country, stopping for lunch at a roadside café and arrive in Penitentes about 3 pm. There is grass on the bare ski slopes which will be the last green we'll see for a couple of weeks. I'm sharing a room with a guy called Jim.

3/2/02 - Penitentes to Campo de Leña

I awake early to a lovely day and after breakfast we hang around again while the baggage is organised for the mules. A ramshackle van drives us to the trailhead and we set off walking under a clear blue sky and baking sun. It is

Luggage being weighed and divided into 30kg loads for the mules.

brutal walking up broken soil and dust but the path is easy and we stop every hour and a half for a rest. Mike, our chief guide, keeps exhorting us to drink lots and keep applying the sunscreen. He's a likeable, lanky young man. Our other guides are a couple – Brian and Carrie. All of them are super fit.

The day is divided into three stages. I was fine on the first stage, but by the last, my right Achilles tendon is hurting badly, my left knee is sore and I have a headache. I look at the others and they all look stronger than I feel and I wonder about my chances of getting to the top.

We reach Campo De Lena and wait an hour for the mules. Once my duffle bag arrives I take a Cuprofen and by the time the meal is ready I begin to feel better. I share Axel's sausage round while we wait for the meal, a chicken/vegetable curry, which is surprisingly good. It looks like Brian will prove to be a good cook.

Before the meal we'd had a lesson in tent erection and I'd decided to bunk with Bill and Pete, the two nice English guys. We sit around chatting and the two older American brothers, Larry and Jim, sing a barbershop duet. The stars come out and we debate whether the planet we can see is Venus and whether the four stars in a kite shape are really the Southern Cross.

It's a warm night, much too hot for my super new sleeping bag, so I sleep on top of my two campamats.

4/02/02 Campo de Lena to Casa de Piedra, 10,500'

I slept surprisingly well – the earplugs really help. An enormous breakfast of huevos revueltos and cereal. My ankle feels much better, but I expect it will get sore during the day. Today I'll take the Cuprofen with me in my pocket. We set off and head up the valley, taking a different route to the mules that have gone along the river. We find out why after 10 minutes or so when we come to a new bridge at a point where the river narrows.

When you walk you have only your thoughts, and doubts about your physical condition assail you. My legs hurt and I worry about being able to keep up, never mind do the climb. I fall to the back so I can go at my own pace and

Our first view of Aconcagua from the Casa de Piedra campsite

avoid the crocodile the others are walking in. Things go through your mind – you become obsessed with the creaks and groans of your legs and chest and an internal dialogue goes on about how you're feeling. If only I'd done more when I was young. The rest of the group go faster than me on the flat – I hope I'll be better going up. If the weather's fine there's no reason I shouldn't be able do the Polish. What will I do though if they say I'm not fit enough? I wonder if everyone else was thinking the same sorts of things.

The Americans all say how pretty the valley is. It's dry desert country and they are obviously much more accustomed to this type of country.

The campsite at Casa De Piedras is spectacular because suddenly there is a view right up the Relinchos Valley to the mountain and you can see the whole of the Polish Route. It's pleasant, on grass, by the side of a stream. There's steak for dinner with mushroom and chilli sauce.

5/2/02 - Casa de Piedra to Base Camp, 12,200'

I didn't sleep as well last night. The ground seemed harder and every time I went off, I must have started snoring because Peter poked me and woke me up. I didn't hear the alarm, but was awake when Mike came round at 6 am and rousted us out.

Each day gets harder, so we need to make an earlier start. Quite soon we have to make the river crossings. I was supposed to have brought neoprene boots but hadn't, so Mike said they'd throw a pair across to me. But the problem was that the wide flood plain forms many channels. It's not called the Braided River for nothing.

I decide to try it in bare feet and so tie my boots round my neck and step in.

The Vacas Valley and the Braided River

Mike had shown us how to use the poles for balance and told us not to look at the flow or we would lose our balance. The water is very cold and I have to be careful not to bang my toes but I make it and put my boots back on. The second and third crossings are more difficult because there are stretches of shingle I have to walk on with bare feet.

We see a guanaco, a relative of the llama and the camel, quite close by on the slope to our left and then another high up and silhouetted against the sky. Just after one o'clock we stop by a stream to fill the water bottles. I've been drinking at least four litres a day. Soon after the mules pass us going down having dropped off our gear. The muleteers are Indian-looking and sit proud.

The day passes. It is harder than the previous two and we have to walk

Larry and Jim doing one of the many river crossings

along the river bed for much of the time. Mike points out a marvellous peak with a snow ridge called El Mano, 'the hand' and gullies where there is ice-climbing in spring.

I hate walking in single file and as we near the campsite, I lose sight of the

Conviviality of the base camp tent

main party. They have either cut up left to the ridge or continued in the stream bed. I decide to climb because it seems the most logical way. I feel good climbing and I am not as out of breath as I'd expected to be. When I reach the crest, I can see the others far below in the river bed, so I return along the ridge to what looks to be the easiest slope and scree down the rubble and sand. Brian, who's been behind me, continues along the ridge and screes straight down into camp.

On arriving the first thing we do is put up the tent. Our camp is on a dry river bed and in a barren moonscape. There is a big dome tent that the previous group erected. Mike says we can have another tent and share in twos rather than threes. So I put up another tent to share with Jeff who also wants to do the Polish. He's young and looks fit now he's recovering from his flu. It's windy here and, as I write sitting on the stones and leaning against my duffle, there is snow in the air.

Brian hasn't been able to find the stoves in the mountains of baggage, so dinner is going to be delayed. I took another Cuprofen today when we stopped for lunch and my ankle and other aches and pains are feeling much better. I still don't know how I'm going to feel higher up or if I have a realistic chance of doing the Polish. It looked great from Casa de Piedra and I'm sure I'd have no problem with it were it at 9,000 rather than 20,000' feet. I was trying to decide if I really liked this kind of thing today – of course you forget the tedium, pain and discomfort and remember the best bits.

The weather isn't too good tonight – lots of cloud and mist and it's spotting with rain. Each evening and morning Brian, assisted by Mike and Carrie, crouches over the stoves and prepares the meal. It's really important we eat well and our success, if any, will owe a lot to Brian's good cooking. Tonight the meal is Mexican. We're sitting around in the dome, chewing the fat, waiting for the hot water to be ready for drinks.

Tomorrow is a rest day to help us acclimatise. The group that is a day ahead of us will do their carry-up to Camp 1 tomorrow. I go to bed early and sleep reasonably well given the stony ground.

6/02/02 - Base camp

I woke at 6.30 am for a pee and then drifted off again until 8.15 when Jeff began to stir. It's a beautiful clear morning and we congregate in the dome tent for cereal followed by pancakes. The other group have left loaded down with monster packs. Jeff gets out his CD player and speakers and the Stones

Breakfast at base camp

blast out across the wasteland that is our home for the next two days.

I set up my campamat against my duffle, change into my shorts and read until 1:00. Then, without giving it much thought, I decide to go for a walk to try out my new boots.

I scramble up the shaley bank directly in front of the camp to the benchland above the river. It is tough scrambling up the loose scree and once on top I continue up the valley, finally crossing the main trail which I decide to follow. I keep climbing, trying to spot tomorrow's route. Then I see some figures coming down and figure it must be Larry and Jim. So I sit against a boulder and wait for them. They say they found good water, so I ask them for some. I haven't brought a water bottle.

As I reach the camp on the way down the third group's gear has arrived on mules. There's going to be quite a lot of people on the mountain, but then it's pretty big. I feel good – my new boots feel comfortable, if very hot, and my breathing and head are fine.

Back at camp Brian is cooking hash browns. So after changing into sandals I begin stocking up – fried potatoes, fried bread and cheese, rye bread and salami. I've never eaten so much on a mountain.

After lunch I get set up again on my lounger. I put my socks on after a while and get a t-shirt to cover my hands because the sun is so strong. I read for a couple of hours or so. People from the third group start to arrive. A bright

A mule train heads off back down the valley

green bird swoops low over the waste-strewn river bed. I notice a patch of green on the hillside, and patches of yellow and orange rock and realise that there is colour in this monochrome desert.

We're in the dome tent, eating hors d'oeuvres. A mild storm is brewing up outside and we have the doors zipped shut to keep out the wind. The small camp table is covered in mugs of soup and pate and bread. People are playing cards. My head is slightly woozy from the little wine I've drunk and the fumes from the stoves. There are two teams cooking simultaneously on four stoves each! I'm sitting near a vent which is creating a gale around my legs, but at least I have some fresh air. The CD player is blasting away and there is quite an atmosphere developing.

Tomorrow we have to wake at 6 and be off by 8.30. I still don't know how heavy a load I'll be carrying. We will leave the loads and come back here again for the night.

I find it difficult to finish the meal. I've lost my appetite and have a mild headache. I'm worried that I may have caught Jeff's virus. He's recovered now but was really ill the first three days. You're super sensitive to how you're feeling. It's difficult being in a big group like this – I much prefer a team of two.

7/02/02 - Carry Base Camp to Camp 1, 15,200'

The walk up to Camp 1 is hard. Mike takes it very steady and I concentrate on flowing, rather than stamping like some of the others. Mike had shown us the rest step in which you rest on the back foot on each step. But it isn't high enough to need to rest like this. So I hang back and go at my own pace. My flowing step consists of trying to make my whole body flow through from one step to the next. The poles really help with this and allow you to glide along with a slight rolling motion like a drunken sailor. The real secret, though, is to plant your foot on what, almost subconciously, you have sussed as the best step. On this pebbly scree this involves concentration and a funny mixture of daintiness and determination.

We pass my high point of yesterday and continue upwards to a small stream where we fill our bottles. The beautiful snow covered mountain to our right we are told is Cerro Zurbriggen. The going is fairly gentle at times and then steep. The mountain is really a slag heap and you're walking on sand, gravel and pebbles of various sizes and shapes. It's hard when it's steep and you have to be careful with your footwork.

Penitentes on the carry to Camp 1

Mike also talked about pressure breathing. It involves an exhaling in an exaggerated manner with a grunt rather like someone in a Japanese martial arts movie. Exhaling like this is supposed to force you to breathe in more deeply. I alternate it with my own breathing technique which involves mentally imagining that you are filling your stomach with air before filling your lungs. Both methods seem to work.

As we reach the headwall of the main valley we turn left up a side valley and have another view of the mountain and the Polish Glacier. We continue up for another hour or so until we reach Camp 1. But Mike says the first group are camping here and we continue upwards for another half an hour until we reach a flat area at 14,920'. Mike points out the route to Camp 3, traversing right

Resting after carry to Camp I

and then left to gain a spiky ridge. Beyond that we can see the upper half of the Polish Glacier. It looks easy angled until the massive bergshrund which you pass on the right where it runs into rocks and forms a chimney pitch. Above it looks steeper and you wouldn't want to fall from that upper slope. But I want to do it and today, since I felt I'd climbed well and never really got out of breath, I begin to believe that I might have a chance of getting up.

We unload our rucksacks. We have each been carrying a food bag which half filled the rucksack, plus our high altitude cold weather inner clothing and technical gear like crampons and axes. I guess it weighed 30-40lbs. We stuff the gear in the duffle bags Mike has carried up for us and pile everything against a rock with a load of stones on top to hold it all down.

After a short rest we head down with Carrie and Brian setting a spanking pace. I more or less keep up which may have been a dumb idea. I get a headache soon after we set off – a delayed reaction maybe or maybe I'm not breathing as deeply as on the climb. It lasts until I reach base camp and take a paracetamol.

My feet have also taken some punishment and I have a bruised toe on each foot. Once back in camp I get my duffle out and slump against it to take off my boots. After a rest I take my wash kit and climb the gravel ridge to the river. I intend to have a proper wash and even wash my hair, but the water is so cold and I am feeling so tired that I have a lick and a promise wash, dash some water on my head and rub my hair with the towel. Back at the tent I change into clean clothes. I am still wearing the yellow check shirt and khaki trousers I've been wearing since I left London so I must have had them on for over a week!

I collect my plate, mug and spoon and hit the dome tent for eats. Tomorrow we'll go all the way back up to Camp 1, this time with the tents and stoves and the rest of our personal stuff. I'm not sure if the packs will be lighter, I hope so. After a night at Camp 1 Mike wants us to do a carry to Camp 3

8/02/02 - Base Camp to Camp 1

We have just reached Camp 1 and I'm writing this snuggled in the tent. It's snowing outside, but the wind has stopped. We left base camp at 11 after packing up the tents. We're sleeping three to a tent again so I'm back with Bill and Pete, the two English blokes I was with at base camp. We had a leisurely breakfast and packed our rucksacks with the rest of our personal gear, plus one third of the tent and an item of communal gear. I got the water bottle, which was light, although later I paid for it. Because my sac was full I strapped my shoes on the outside.

Mike set an unbelievably slow pace which was good. I hung back and took the last place in the line again. The others were doing the rest step, so I tended to catch up as they bunched up on the steep sections and would then rest on my sticks until a gap had developed. We stopped for a rest at the stream and I sat on my rucksack and had something to eat. We stopped again for lunch and the Brits were ribbed again for grabbing the lightest food bags when they were being allocated the night before. They had all been laid on the ground and people were comparing weight by lifting one bag after another. I joined them and Jeff and Steve pointed out that the Brits were at it again and I realised the other three people grabbing bags were fellow Brits.

At Camp I we managed to get the tent up before it began to snow

Today we continued up to the lower Camp I and met up with Pancho, the chief guide of group 1. We took our packs off and I suddenly noticed one of my shoes was missing. I'd strapped it on really tightly but it must have been pushed off at one of the rest stops. Mike said we'd ask Jim's party, the third group, to look out for it on their way down tomorrow. So there is a chance they'll find it. Otherwise I'll have to do the eighteen mile hike out in my plastic double boots. I almost wanted to go back for it there and then. It wouldn't have made sense and it doesn't affect my chances of getting to the top anyway. It's just that I hate losing things.

Shortly after that we got to the stream and everyone was filling their water bottles, I decided to fill the communal water container and carry it up to the higher camp where we'd left the kit. It took a while to fill with the plastic measuring jug and the others went on. It must have weighed about 30lbs. I was able to walk about 20 paces then I had to stop, rest and change hands. Brian caught me up as I reached camp and took over for the last hundred yards.

It started to snow and we had to put up the tent in a gale. We were camped on a flat stony area on the ridge. The three of us worked well together and got the tent up after a false start when we realised we hadn't left enough room for the vestibule between the tent and a large rock we had decided to huddle behind. We had to excavate huge boulders to tie the tent down. We climbed in and as I write, I still have all my outer clothes on and feel chilly. We've been out once for hot water to make packet soup. It's seven o'clock and we're waiting for the main meal to be cooked. It's cold but it's getting snug in the tent.

9/02/02 Camp 1 to Camp 3

I had a fairly good night. I tried to drink whenever I woke but the water was very cold. In fact, one bottle froze. We get up at 7 and I try to drink as many mugs of hot water as I can . I've taken to drinking camomile tea. They've forgotten to bring up the regular tea and it wasn't very good anyway.

Breakfast is rice porridge which is too sweet for me. I nearly puke, which would be a disaster since I'm worried I haven't drunk enough and don't want to lose any liquid.

The climb is the hardest so far and I am tired by the time we get to Camp 2. I have an altitude headache and, when we stop to rest, Steve Lee kindly gives me an Ibruprofen which begins to make a difference.

We have a break here. Mike says he wants to divide the party into two groups. He says we will have a much tougher day when we go for the summit so we should start going faster. He wants the guys doing the Polish, me and Jeff, plus any others who want to go fast, to join the first group. He says Steve Lee should be up for the faster pace. I think I'm not sure I am.

I realise it is a test so I stay behind Mike and match my pace to his. I concentrate on trying to keep my rhythm and to breathe properly. But it seems endless and at times I wonder if my body will be able to keep going. My breathing is good. I don't get out of breath and am able to practice the deep breathing techniques.

The traverse to the needle-shaped rock seems endless. Absent-mindedly I allow a yard or two gap to develop between Mike and myself. I think about changing my pace but am lethargically stuck in the slow rest pace. I know I can catch Mike, but don't make the effort. The gap widens and then I feel Steve Lee on my shoulder and he says, "I'm coming through". He's by far the strongest member of the group. Normally I let anyone pass me, but for some reason I speed up. It feels like changing gear. I can feel Steve trying to pass then changing his mind. "It's like those bastards who accelerate when you try and pass them on the freeway", he complains. I laugh and say, "I didn't feel like letting you through". "That's the sort of attitude you need for the Polish", he says.

Penitente on the way to Camp 2

We finally reach the needle rock, but instead of stopping for a rest, Mike keeps going. I'm dizzy with the lack of oxygen and have to concentrate to keep up.

We have a good long rest on the top and I watch a couple of climbers on the upper part of the Polish. They seem very small, so it must be bigger than it looks. Anyway, the main thing is I've passed the test, or so I believe. We shoot down at a great lick and when we reach camp I am presented with my shoe. So I'll have shoes to walk out in. But I've also been worried that I can't find the thick socks I've been saving for the summit. Oh dear I'm not having a very good time with my kit!

The three of us are crushed up in the tent. Peter has finally found the camera and notebook he'd been ranting about for the last hour – turning the kit over and making us lift our camper mats. It's not easy keeping track of stuff in a crowded tent when you have to move it every other day.

10/02/02 Camp 1 to Camp 2 16,500'

We had a lie in until 8.45. We have an easy day today to Camp 2. I slept well after playing scrabble with Peter and Bill.

Jeff has offered to lend me a pair of thick socks and when I go over to get

The Polish Route from Camp 3: at this stage in perfect condition

them, he asks me if I still want to go for the Polish. I say yes. He says he's not sure. Partly it's because he's keen to stay with the main group. He's also worried about trying to climb at 19,500'. I feel OK here at 15,000,' at rest, but as soon as I do anything strenuous, like just getting in and out of the tent, I get out of breath. It's new territory for both of us.

It's Sunday today and I have a vision of reading the papers at the kitchen table at Leveret Croft with a cup of coffee and I wonder what's the attraction of climbing high. Maybe I should forget the Himalayas, or at least register this doubt now while it's fresh in my mind.

We've just made it to Camp 2. We put the tents up straight away before having a rest and anchor them down with big rocks. I'm in the tent and it's snowing outside. Less than an hour ago when we arrived, it was sunny and warm. I've got the tent to myself. Bill and Pete have gone to another tent to play cards and so I'm taking advantage of the spaciousness to spread out. I've borrowed Bill's camparest seat to sit up in and am now waiting for Mike to get the stoves fired-up for hot drinks.

On the walk up we went faster than yesterday and did it in two hours rather than three. I felt fresher today, and, although I really liked the slow pace, could have gone faster. I guess I'm acclimatising. I stayed at the back on the walk up, which I like. Steve Lee said my pace is steady. So people like to sit in behind

Cairn near Camp 2, looking back north to Cerro Zurbriggen/Fitzgerald

me and I can't always get the rear slot.

One slight disaster this morning when we were packing – I could only find one of three pairs of clean inner socks that I'd been saving. I've obviously got a thing with socks on this trip. It discomforted me and I had to tell myself that it wasn't important. I'd just have smelly feet!

I'm sitting in the tent, recovering from having spilt a cup of tea everywhere. There was a break in the weather and I was just congratulating myself on having walked down to fill my water bottles from melt water under ice. Having downed one cup of tea, I'd gone for a second and I was just settling down to read when Peter's stuff sac rolled across the slope the tent is pitched on and knocked over my mug. I've had to use half my remaining toilet paper mopping up. But now I'm settled, the tent is back to normal, and I'm eating my supper – pasta primavera – and have cold water to drink instead of tea.

11/02/02 Camp 2 to Camp 3, 17,800'

We have made it to Camp 3 and I'm breathless having just helped put up the tent and get my kit organised. It's an exposed site on a shoulder directly below the Polish Glacier. We'll spend three nights here acclimatising – a rest day tomorrow, then a carry to Camp 4, our highest camp, at White Rocks on the normal route. Hopefully we'll spend only two nights at this high camp if

Another view of the Polish Route from Camp 3

we can summit the first day.

This morning, I managed a good breakfast with three mugs of assorted drinks plus hash browns. I didn't find the walk up too difficult and made it here in good style in the first group, so I'm in good spirits. The sun is out, but it's very cold, -12°C, way below freezing.

I guess we'll be spending a lot of time in bed tomorrow. I've read two books to date and I'm on my third, but having to share it with Bill. We got in the tent when it started to snow and played cards. Despite taking great pains to make a level site, we're sliding into a hole full of lumpy rocks. We're resigned to having to shift the tent if it stops snowing. We also need to fix the guys so the fly's not touching. Earlier we were congratulating ourselves on having got the tent up in double quick time. I can't believe we cocked it up so comprehensively.

We've managed to rebuild the tent platform. We had to undo most of the guys, and by lifting up the tent on one side, managed to shovel gravel in to level the site. I really envy the guys their blow-up thermarests. They're much more comfortable than my campamats, even though I have two.

12/02/02 - Camp 3, 17,800'

It's nine o'clock in the morning and I'm feeling really grotty with the altitude. I had a difficult night. I was cold and one of my hip joints got very sore. It was difficult getting up to pee, and even harder to drink enough. I drank the litre I'd kept in my sleeping bag to stop it freezing, but it wasn't nearly enough and I have a raging headache this morning. I've taken a paracetamol but it hasn't done any good. I need liquid, but the guides still haven't got the stoves going to melt the snow.

In the night the inside of the tent got completely covered in hoar frost from our breathing and every time one of us moved, it sent a cascade of the crystals down on us. "Why do we do it?" I'm asking myself. And if it's this bad here, what will it be like at the high camp?

It's now mid-morning and I've managed to drink four mugs of hot water and eat a bowl of cereal. They'd cooked polenta, but I couldn't face it. My headache has gone at last and I'm no longer feeling nauseous.

Each day Carrie takes a reading of the oxygen saturation in our blood and our heart rate. Today mine is good – 86%, which surprises me since I felt so ill. I've also managed my morning crap! I'm not sure what the temperature was last night, but it must have been at least -20°C.

Pete and I at Camp 3. Cerro Fitzgerald in background

The first party have left on their carry to high camp. It looked hard work. Tomorrow we'll do our carry and return here to sleep. It's after midday and I spend an hour sorting my gear. I check that my crampons fit and that I can grasp my axe in my thick gloves. I try my gaiters and realise they require a special technique to get them on over double boots. A group is playing scrabble and others are checking gear too. I'm not sure how Brian feels about doing the Polish. I imagine he's wishing we were doing it today since the weather is fine – strong sun and little wind. I hope it keeps fine for the next three days.

I spend the rest of the day sitting around drinking water and reading. Then when Mike gets back he takes us for crampon and ice-axe practice. I hadn't been intending to do it. I still feel grotty and think it is optional, but Mike makes it clear I should join in, so I do. You can always learn new things. I still don't know if I'll be doing the Polish, but am feeling a bit better after a day's rest.

It's evening and snowing hard outside. I'm writing this in the tent muffled up in my strawberry duvet. We ate outside. Brian announced it as 'noodle surprise' consisting of tuna, soya, 'fresh' dried peas and noodles. It was surprisingly good. Three is too many for a tent this size and it's hard making room for each other. It would have been a lot easier two to a tent.

Tomorrow we have to carry to our high camp, which is going to be a hard day. The guides have a satellite 'phone, which they charge out at $5 a minute. One or two people made calls tonight and got answering machines. I thought

Carrie measuring heart rate and the oxygen saturation in our blood

Mike and Carrie at Camp 3

I'd wait until after our summit attempt. But I regret not having remembered to order flowers or send a card for Valentine's Day. Other people, more far-sighted than me, have placed orders with florists.

13/02/02 Carry Camp 3 to Camp 4, 19,200'

We woke about 7.30 after a reasonable night. I managed to drink some water in the night. I had two water bottles in bed with me and I was praying neither broke.

It's now 4.30 p.m. and we've been up to our high camp, left gear and come back. We did the climb very quickly in two and a half hours with only one rest. I found it hard but I was OK.

It has snowed every afternoon for the past four days and the Polish is no longer in condition. The three groups are together now at Camp 4 and of the original thirty people, I think I'm the only one who wants to do it still. Given the deep snow, I'd have a difficult time. Brian, the guide who'd be leading it, said he didn't think it would go. Mike asked me, did it bother me or was getting to the summit the important thing. He told me that Jeff had decided he preferred the better odds of getting to the top on the normal route. I said that for me, the route was important, but if I can't do the Polish, I'll try to get up with the main group.

Now I'm feeling grotty again from the altitude and am sure I'm going to feel bad on summit day. The main thing that will stop us though is a change in the weather. It's been great now for two weeks, with bright, clear mornings and the bad weather rolling in at 3 or 4 o'clock in the afternoon. Today, the wind was from the east and there were clouds first thing. The worry is that we'll get bad weather and strong winds when we hit the summit ridge and be unable to do the last half mile or so. I've just been to get another litre of water and need to force myself to drink. It's difficult pouring down five litres a day, but I need to try.

It's amazing how lethargic you feel at high altitude. I've been telling myself for the past half-hour to get out of the tent and check the guys in case a storm blows up. Much of the walk today was on snow. Mike broke trail and I followed and then Steve Lee. He said I should stamp more to make the step. I disagreed. My job is to make sure I don't demolish the step and, by stepping cleanly, to consolidate it.

Fairly near the top, Mike announced 'only ten minutes to go', and the last few hundred feet or so were tough. It hasn't snowed yet today, so maybe there is a chance of doing the Polish. Now, of course, I doubt I'm strong enough for the twenty-two hours it's supposed to take. You have to descend in a long slanting traverse back to get onto the glacier. Then there is 2-3,000' of steep snow with a steeper section to get past the bergshrund. Finally you have the long ridge to the summit. On the normal route, which we join at White Rocks, you don't have to descend. There is just a long traverse across to the Caneleta.

I have just been out to tighten the guys and have powdered my feet and changed into clean dry socks. Bill is playing cards in one of the other tents and Pete is in here reading. I've read all three books Bill, Pete and I brought, but the trip is nearly over, I hope.

14/02/02 Move Camp 3 to Camp 4 19,500'

I'm lying in the tent at our high camp, which smells of shit and is on clay, which we've mashed up with our boots. The walk up wasn't so bad but we've come up 1,800' and I've not acclimatised to this new altitude. All three of us found it difficult just erecting the tent. I've got a bad headache and have taken a Cuprofen, which has helped. But I've drunk all my water and badly need more. Mike has pitched the cook tent a long way away. They're melting snow now, and will bring it round, I hope.

Pancho's group were due to summit today, but they had high winds and extreme cold this morning and so decided not to go. I don't know if it will be the same tomorrow. I've decided definitely not to do the Polish Route - it isn't in condition. So I'll be going with the others to try the normal route tomorrow, weather permitting.

I've spent the last hour getting dressed in my high altitude clothes. Two vests, a shirt, and the fleece trousers Colin lent me over running tights. I plan to sleep in my warm clothes so I'm ready in the morning.

Brian calls that the hot water is ready. I manage to drink a mug and a half. Then Mike calls me into the tent for a talk. He'd consulted Pancho who said he wouldn't be prepared to guide the Polish Route in its current condition. I say I'd give the normal route a shot, which would be a big achievement, given how grotty I am feeling this evening.

Mike came over and we all crammed into our tent for a summit pep talk. Unless it's too cold or windy, the plan is to wake at four and leave for the summit at six.This evening the weather is gorgeous – bright sun and mild. And we haven't had the usual snow this evening. I'm not sure how I feel about the climb and my own physical state. I'm disappointed about not being able to do the Polish Route. I've been thinking about it for thirty years since I read a book by the first ascentionists. They were six young Poles who, in 1934, designed and made their own equipment and then climbed the route Alpine style. It was one of the books that inspired me to be a climber.

Now I'm worried about whether I'll even get up the normal route. I guess I know I'll keep going. I'm nowhere near as sprightly as I was in my thirties, but I've always had lots of stamina.

They have five guides between 14 clients – six from the first group and eight from ours. There ought to be enough guides to deal with people who need to go down.There is also talk about going down to Plaza de Mulas tomorrow

Eleven of us crammed into our tent for a summit pep talk from Mike

rather than camping here another night. Either way tomorrow is going to be a very hard day.

15/02/02 Summit 22,800'

We were woken at 4am and I stayed in my pit until 5. I'd taken a Cuprofen before going to sleep which had reduced my headache. But I hadn't been able to eat because I felt sick. I'd put vitamin C in my water bottle and the acid made things worse. But despite this, I had a good night's sleep. Brian, one of the guides, had given me a Diamox tablet. Larry has been taking Diomox and said one of the side effects was that he was peeing nine times a night. So I decided not to take it.

We set off at 6.15. It's dark and very cold. Even in the super double boots and heavy socks, my feet feel cold. My hands are cold too. Despite a lot of discouragement from Mike who didn't want people to use poles I decide to take mine.

I keep up with Mike on the walk up to the Independencia hut, which is just under half way. He'd said that when we got there he would split the party into a fast group with a good chance of summiting, and a slower group with a lower chance. So I am determined to keep up and make the necessary impression.

We have a long break at the hut. It's a tiny wooden A-frame. Some of the

Independencia hut, 20,800'

boards have gone and it's full of snow. From there we climb a steep snow slope and then begin the long traverse of the Gran Alcarreo. It's there you get strong winds. But today it's fine.

Mike ropes up five of us in the fast group. There is a 6,000' drop to Plaza de Mulas, but the chance of one of us tripping and sliding all the way must be

Traverse of the Gran Acarreo and the Caneleta up the gully to the left

At the start of Caneleta

negligible. A consequence of being roped is that you can't go at your own pace. You can't even stop and take photographs. The Caneleta is quite different to what I'd expected. I had read that it was a 1,000' steep gully. We climb the Caneleta in a single slanting leftward traverse towards the summit.

Mike with the summit cross multi wrapped in flags and offerings

Mike, Steve, Bill, Jeff, Jim and me on the summit 22,800'

Mike sets a steady slow pace but I find that with the altitude I have to stop for a couple of seconds every 20 or 30 steps. Although I only need to rest a moment it must be frustrating for Jeff who is in front of me and gets pulled short.

We reach some rocks and suddenly find ourselves on the top. It is great to know we've made it safely and that there was no more ascent.

We had been told the climb would take six to ten hours and we had done it in seven. So we were fairly fast. There is a small cross on the top and a metal box with a visitors' book. I use Mike's satellite 'phone for the first time and telephone Scharlie. The line is fantastically good and she is obviously thrilled to hear I'd made it. .

We are roped again on the way down and Jim, who is directly in front of me, trips three times in the Caneleta. They aren't bad trips and he is quite safe, but crossing the Gran Acarreo, the only potentially dangerous place on the whole route, Jim keeps pulling me off my feet. Again I don't think it is dangerous, but if he does fall I don't feel that I stand much chance of stopping him. So I try to go at my own pace and slow him down by pulling the rope between us. Maybe it is my fault for going too slowly! I try telling Jim but he just tugs on the rope. (This was the only time on the trip when I felt annoyed.) Mike tells me to chill out and I decide he's right and I'm making a fuss.

We spent an hour on the summit – plenty of time for self-portraiture

We unrope once we reach safer ground and we each go at our own pace and finally reached the camp. I have a word with a Lithuanian called Mikas who I'd made friends with in Mendoza. He's in the third group which has just done their move to high camp. He looks tired and is obviously anxious about summitting tomorrow. Tomorrow, we do our big carry down to Plaza de Mulas and the following day the eighteen mile walk out.

16/02/02 Camp 4 to Plaza de Mulas, 13,800'

I'm packed and waiting to begin the walk down. My pack weighs a ton. We're carrying twice as much as on the ascent, since we always did two carries. In addition to all our gear, I have two large duffels and half the tent. It's very cold, and my hands are frozen. I'm sitting with my rucksack propped against a rock so I don't have to lift it onto my back again. This is one of the things you get used to when you're with a party - having to wait for people.

The way down to Plaza de Mulas is pebbly shale – it's like walking on ball bearings. The paths are steep and hurt your knees. Thank God for sticks. Rather than take it directly I use the zigzag paths which are much less steep. But it means I am slower and arrive after the others. It doesn't sound important now I write this and it was the right decision to take it steady. But having

Starting the descent loaded down with 60lb+ packs

spent two weeks keeping up with the group it becomes ingrained and feels a wrench letting go of this basic discipline. Mike said later that lots of older guides now regret running down steep slopes with huge loads since they now have bad knees.

It is great reaching the Patagonicas tent and just sitting down. I take my boots

S5,000' of unrelenting descent to Plaza de Mulas

off and pamper my feet with powder and change into the light shoes I'll wear from here. We're sitting in a tent in Plaza de Mulas, eating pizza while I scribble these notes. We're discussing how to round off the trip – whether to go to the beach, or stick to the original plan of spending a night in Pentitentes and a night in Santiago. The young guys want to go straight to the beach, the older guys want to stick to the original plan, shower, eat, and move out in an orderly way.

We have just reached the 'Hotel' – a massive refuge – at Plaza de Mulas, and have ordered beers. The walk over here wasn't easy in my deck shoes and I slipped on the shale and cut my hand. We're bunking four to a room. I'm with Pete and Bill again, plus Steve Lee.

We've decided to go to Penitentes tomorrow. Then the four of us may hire a car and go off exploring. We had a beer and a pleasant meal. The dinner had been booked for eight and I was starving. The guides had stayed back at Plaza de Mulas to organise the gear and to wait for the last of the group. So I joined Pancho's group to meet new people. In fact, the guides arrived only half-an-hour late so the rest of the group didn't have to wait long. Tomorrow I have to walk eighteen miles in my 'deck' shoes!

Some of the shanty town of tents at Plaza de Mulas

17/02/02 Plaza de Mulas to Penitentes

I had a good night's sleep and breakfast at 8 in the hotel. I try to telephone Scharlie but could only get the answering machine. I'm feeling fine about walk out, despite light-weight shoes, because we'll be carrying virtually nothing. I've forced my sleeping-bag into the bottom of my rucksack. It wasn't easy because it fluffs up to a huge size. But now I can use the stuff-sac as a day-pack to carry my jacket, water bottle, a little food and this notebook and pen – all I need on walk-out.

We've just got down to the path entrance. It took just over six hours. The Horcones Valley is more interesting than the Vacas. There are lots of cliffs and great views. I'm used to this dry mountain desert environment now and

Gear for a Jagged Globe expedition via Paza de Mulas - poor bastards!

through sunglasses the colours are vibrant. Without them the scene is washed out by the strong sunlight.

But it's marvellous to get down to where it is vegetated and green. We see a hawk and lots of greenfinch. There are a group of young people sitting by a lake. They must have walked up from the trail-head. It looks nice in the sun but there is a cool breeze and it feels like Autumn and the end of the season. All the group are in good humour, knowing we've all made it.

The pace is brisk for the last couple of miles and there is some competition from Steve and Bill to get down first.

Climbing is surprisingly competitive. I'd argued with Bill that it wasn't, but that's nonsense. But the competition is subtle and is as much with oneself, the mountain and the weather as with the other people in the group. In an all male party it sometimes seems that there is a lot of testosterone flying around. All in all though, ego wasn't a problem in this group. All the clients were experienced mountaineers and good walkers and the guides were relaxed and very competent.

Last view of Aconcagua from near the end of the walk down

Sitting on the bridge near the end of the trail I am able to contemplate the trip as a whole. We were lucky with the weather on the whole trip. On the summit day it was cold, but if you kept moving this wasn't a problem. It would obviously have been much tougher had we had high winds. Although I couldn't have gone any faster, I felt strong and could have kept going with wind and snow. On a guided trip like this though the guides would have pulled the plug if the weather had turned bad.

I hadn't done the route I'd wanted to do, but that's just tough. I guess it's unlikely I'll come here again. Coming on an organised expedition enabled me to climb a mountain I'd wanted to do for the past thirty years. The big difference between a guided trip and the climbing I'm used to concerns decision making. Planning the trip at home and having to make decisions on the trip itself is a major part of my enjoyment. Surprisingly, I don't believe that there is much difference in the degree of risk. There are guide-books and maps that make the planning straightforward and, once on the mountain, the path is so well trodden that it is hard to get lost.

I consciously tried throughout the trip to think for myself, to take responsibility for every move. But I can see that as I get older I could easily get used to the luxury of having it all laid on for me and then the way I've always been climbing would begin to look impossible.

18/2/02 Penitentes to Santiago

Penitentes, the ski-resort where we began our trip, seems much more comfortable and warm than on our arrival two weeks ago. We arrived much too late to make the trip to Santiago so it was just as well Mike changed the plan.

We stop at Puente del Inca for hamburgesas completas, which are absolutely delicious. A natural stone arch forms a spectacular bridge over the Rio Horcones. The slender arch looks about a hundred feet wide and a hundred and fifty feet above the river. I regret I've finished all my film and regret it again when we begin the amazing decent into Chile. The bus driver stops and we can look down and see curve after curve falling away 2000' in less than a mile.

We develop a puncture in one of the rear double tyres and have to drive at 25mph for the next two hours until we reach Los Andes. We sit under trees outside a café while we wait for the tyre to be fixed. Back in the van, on our way to Santiago, Pete says that, when they get back home having been away on holiday, he and his wife list the three best and three worst things of the trip.

For me, the three best were being with a great group of clients and guides, doing the whole trip in good style and summiting. The three worst were not doing the Polish, the walk down to Plaza de Mulas and having to be roped on summit day. Altogether, though, it was a successful and enjoyable trip. All ten clients traversed the mountain and eight got to the summit. But more important than this the expedition had a genuinely good feel about it.

www.ingramcontent.com/pod-product-compliance
Lightning Source LLC
LaVergne TN
LVHW052301100826
845147LV00001B/108

* 9 7 8 1 9 1 2 4 6 0 0 8 3 *